Sacred Heart

A Coloring Book Inspired by Sacred Heart Art

by Nicole Cappelleri

Copyright © Nicole Cappelleri 2015. All rights reserved.

No part of this Book may be reproduced or transmitted in any form or by any means, electronic or mechanical, including photocopying, recording or by any information storage and retrieval system, without written permission from the author.

All enquiries please email NCHarleyBooks@gmail.com

The author can be found at ActivePatience.com

Get your free gift here...

ActivePatience.com/sacred-heart

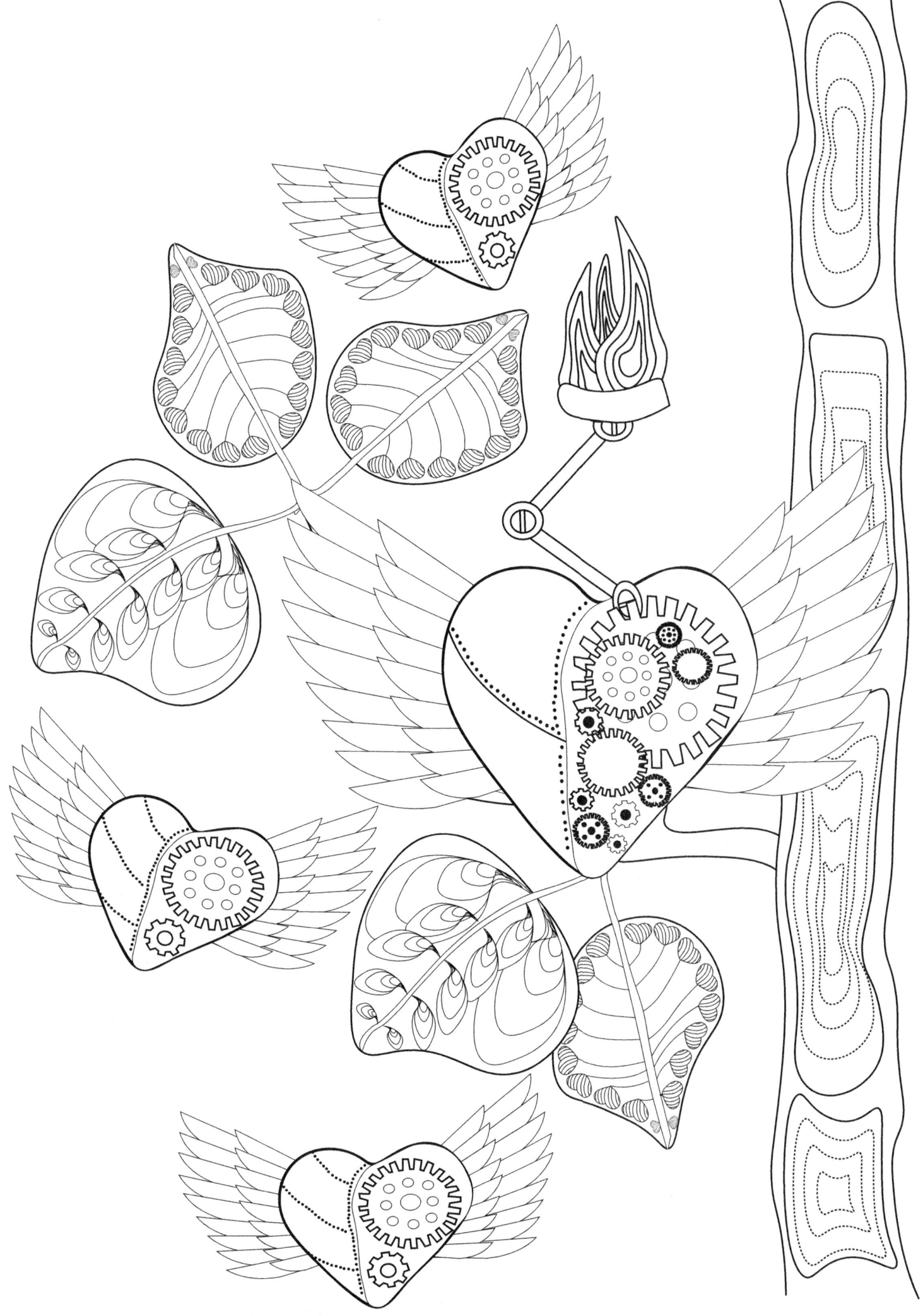

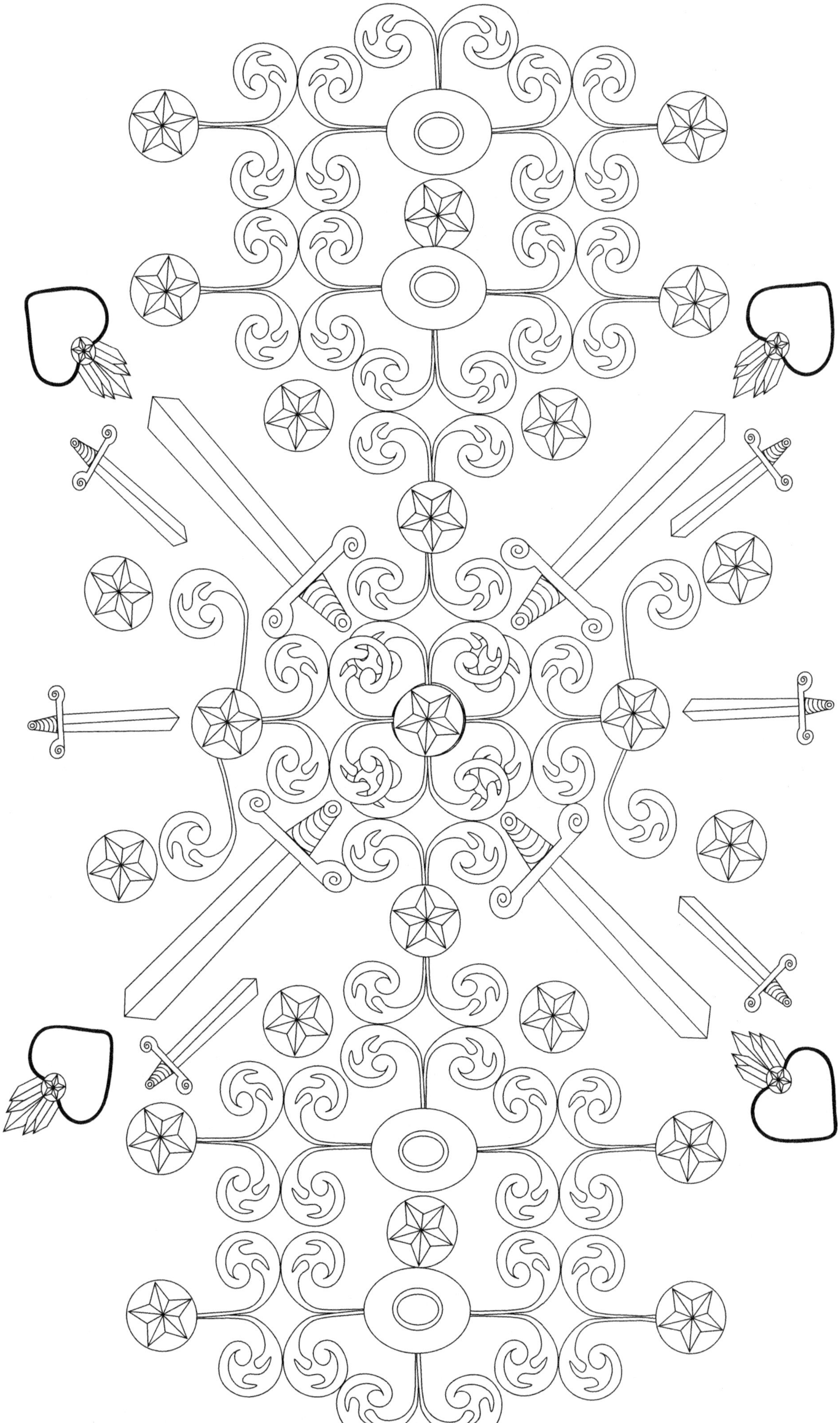

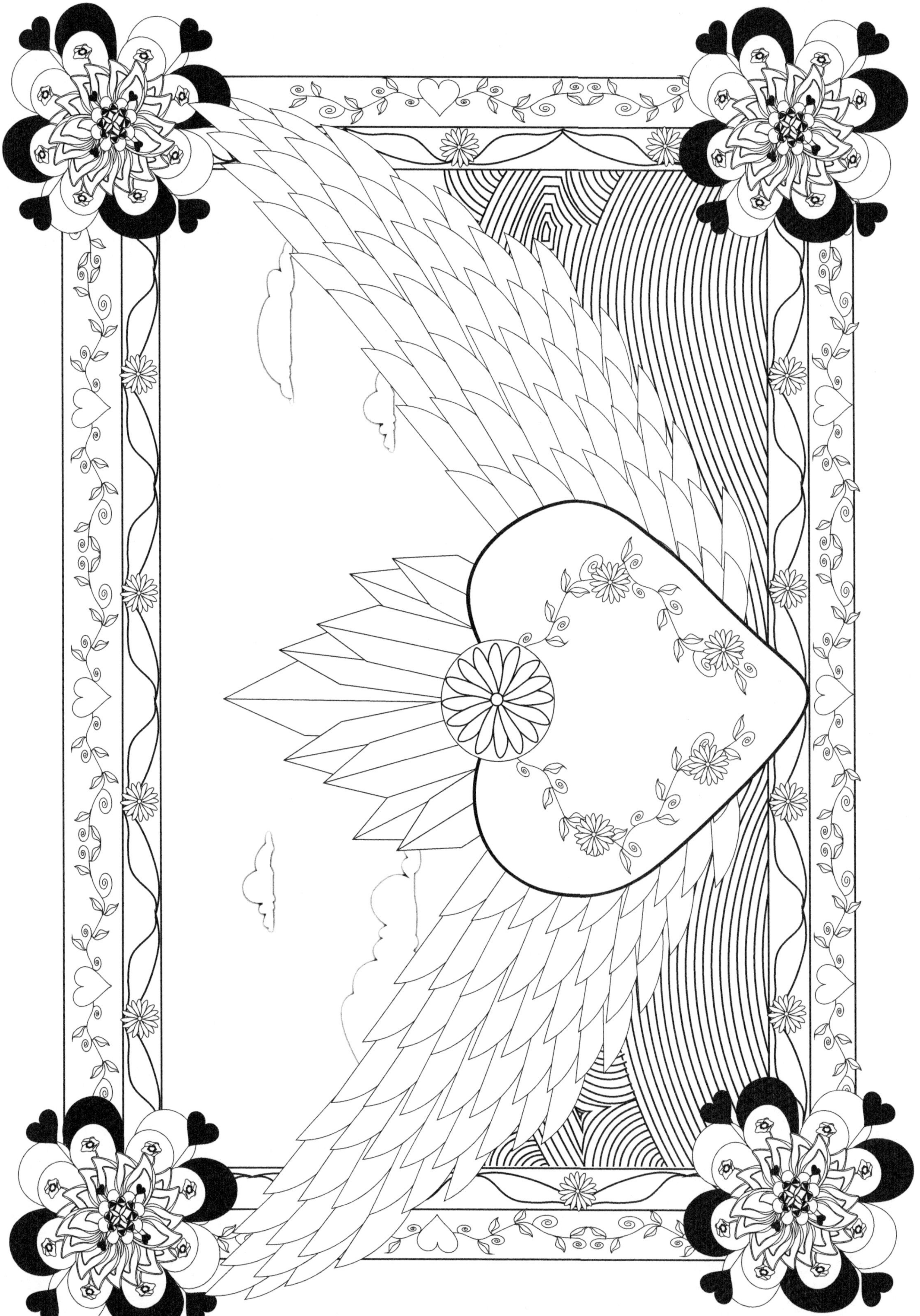

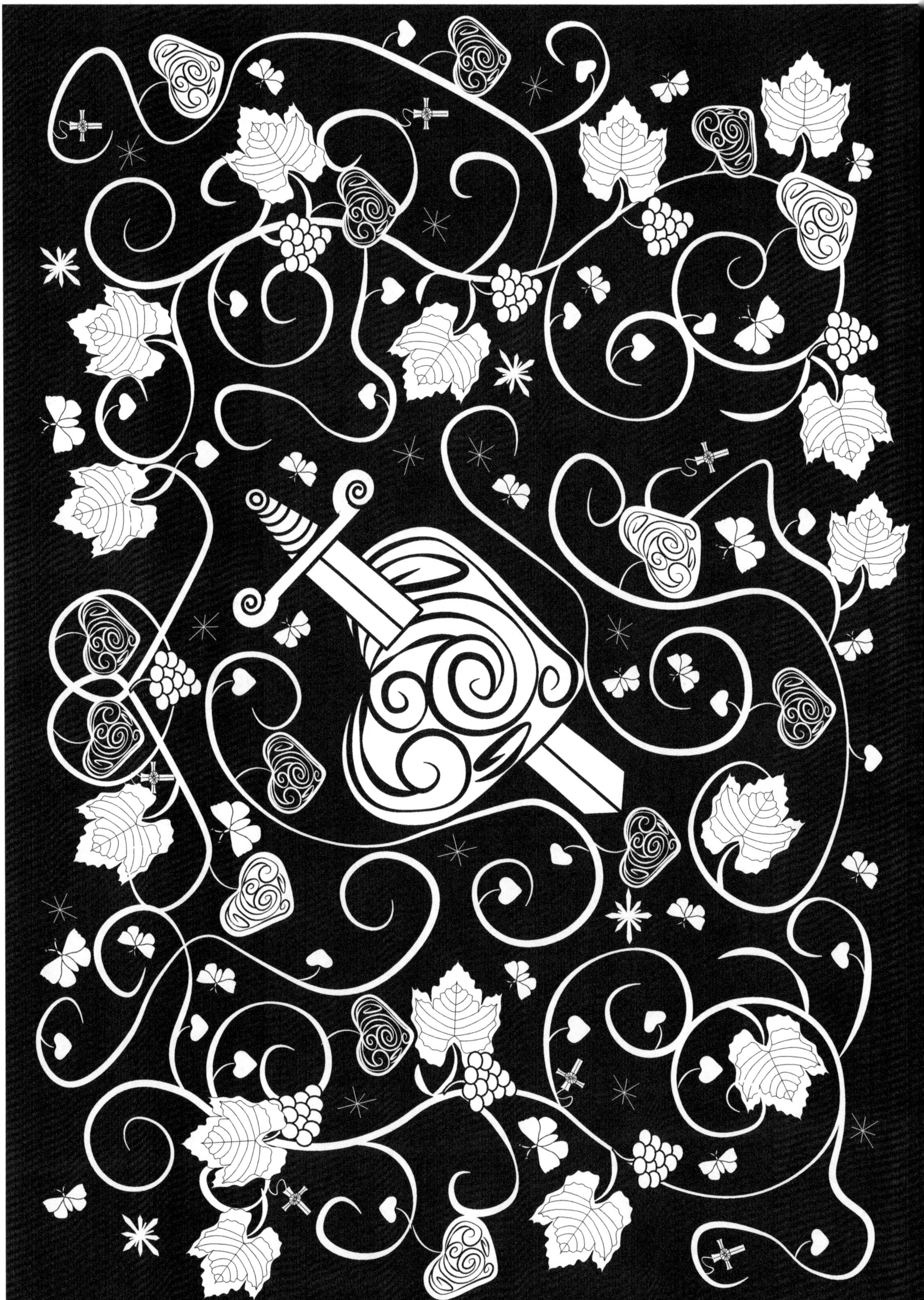

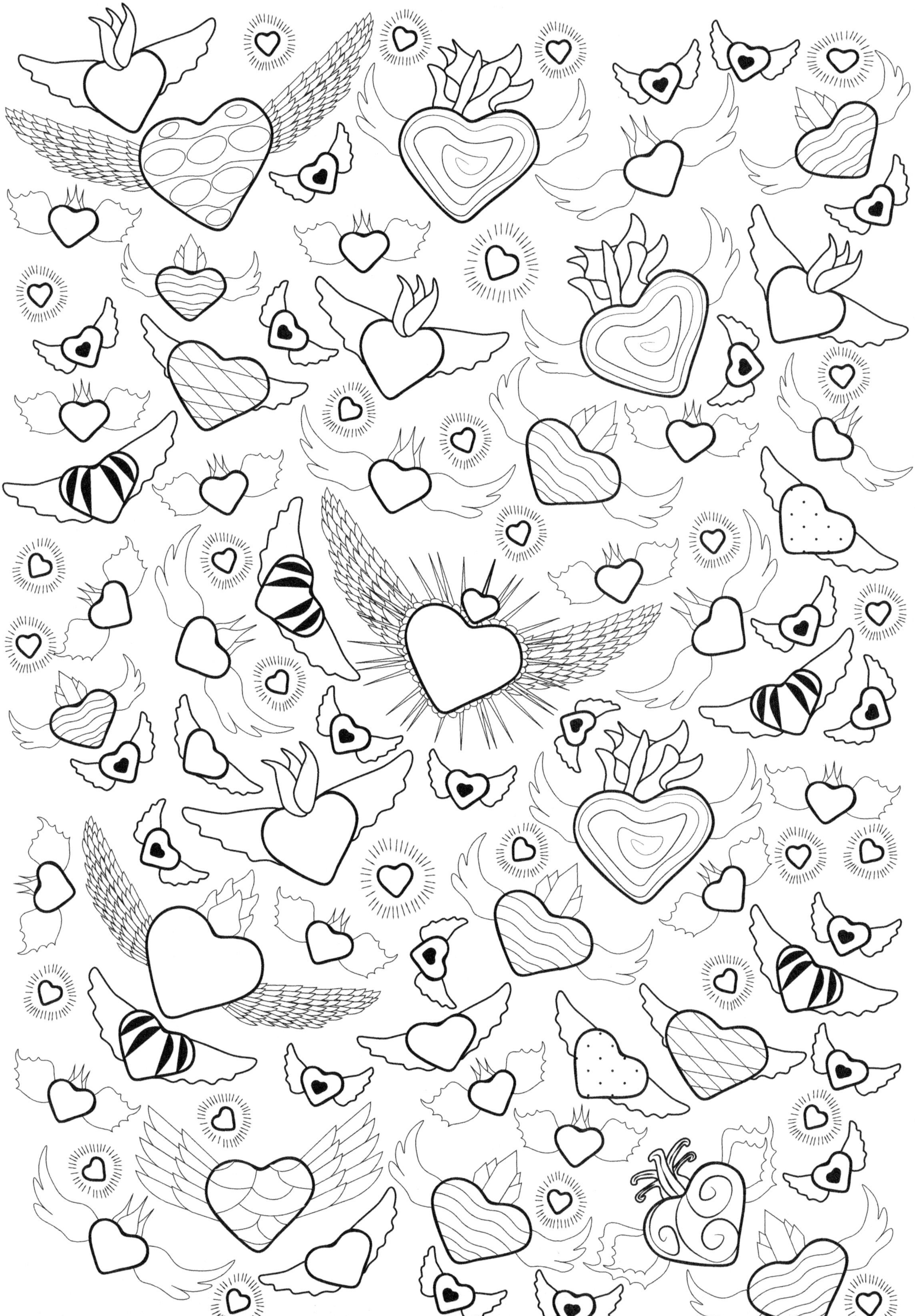

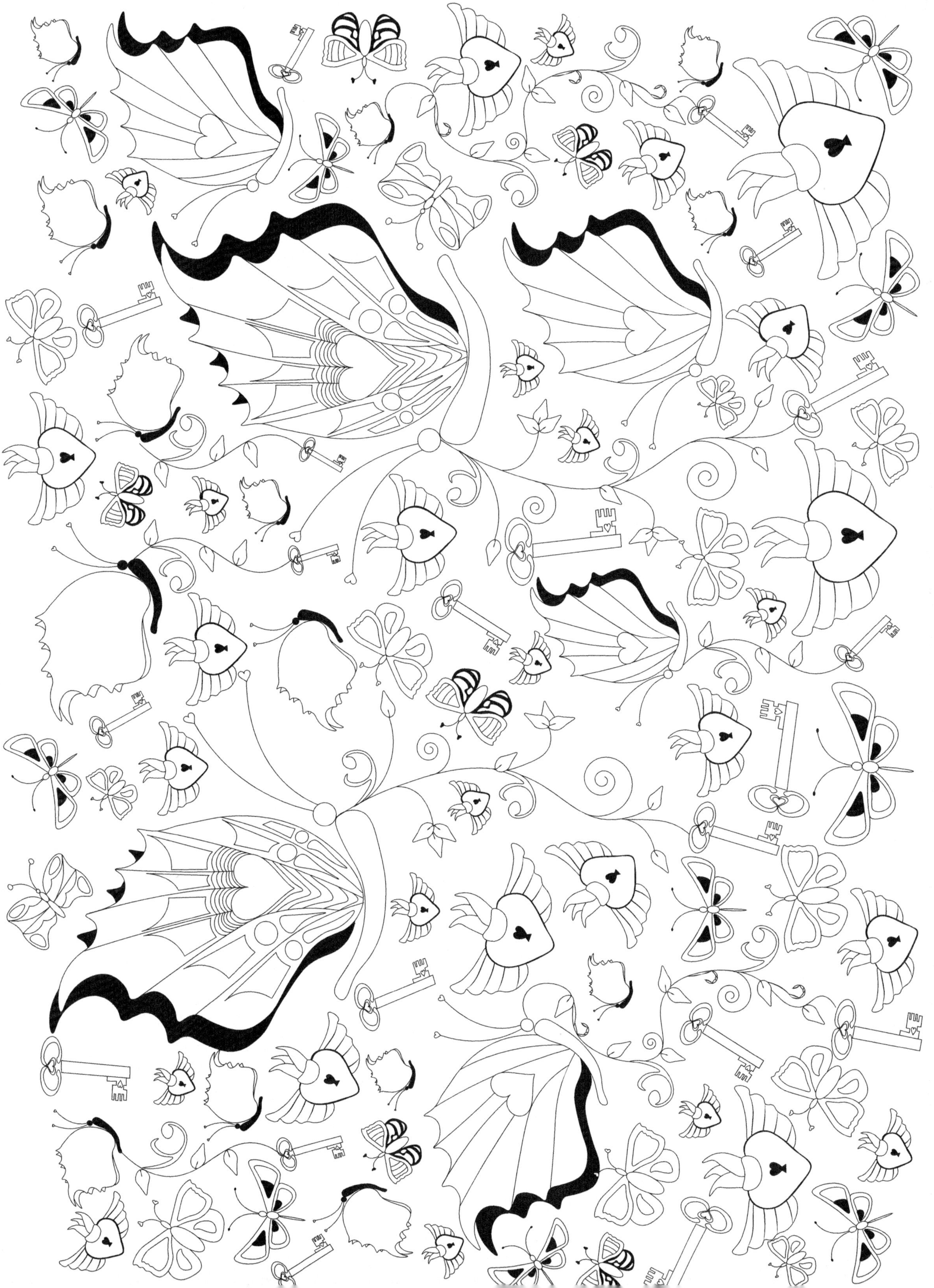

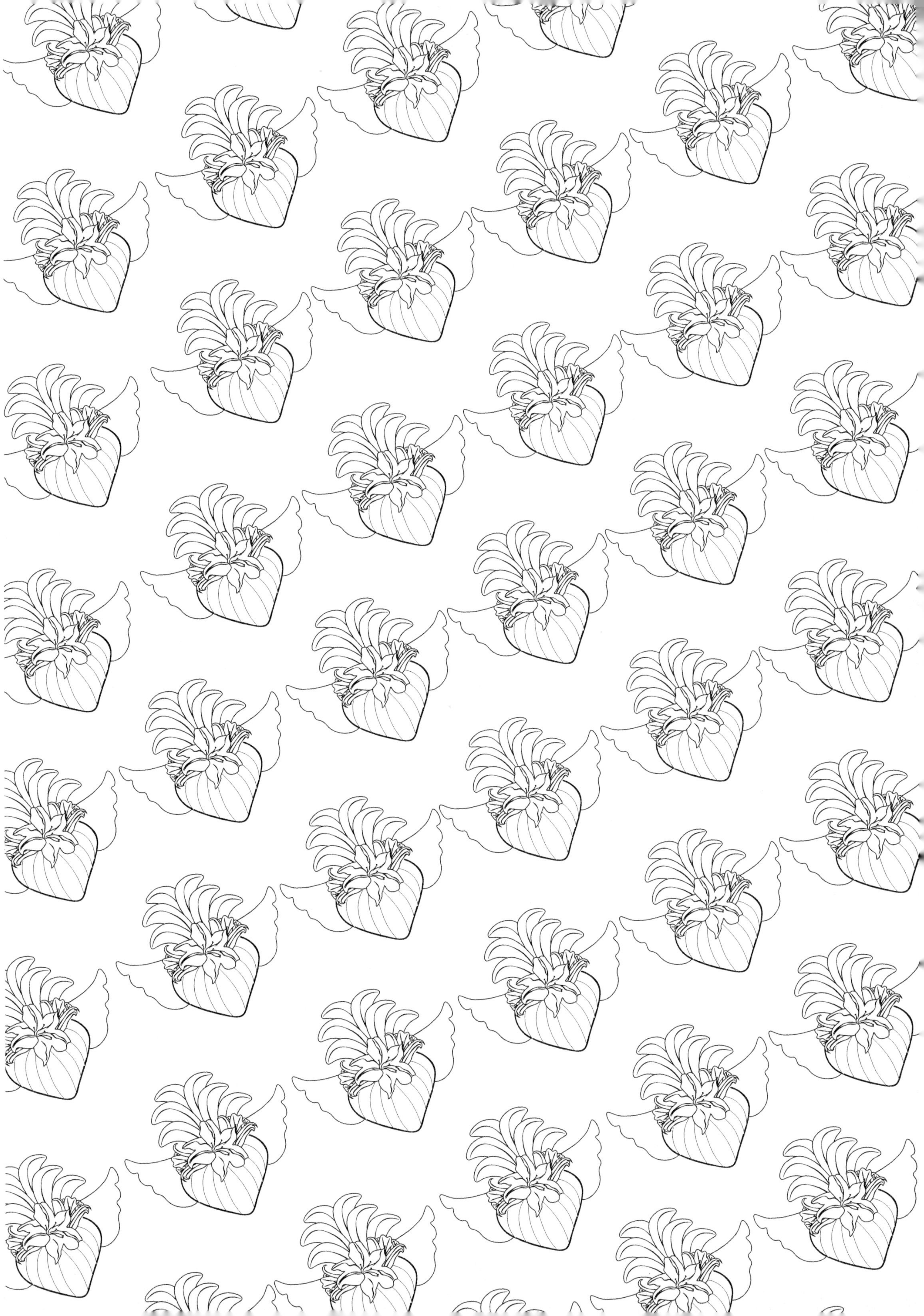

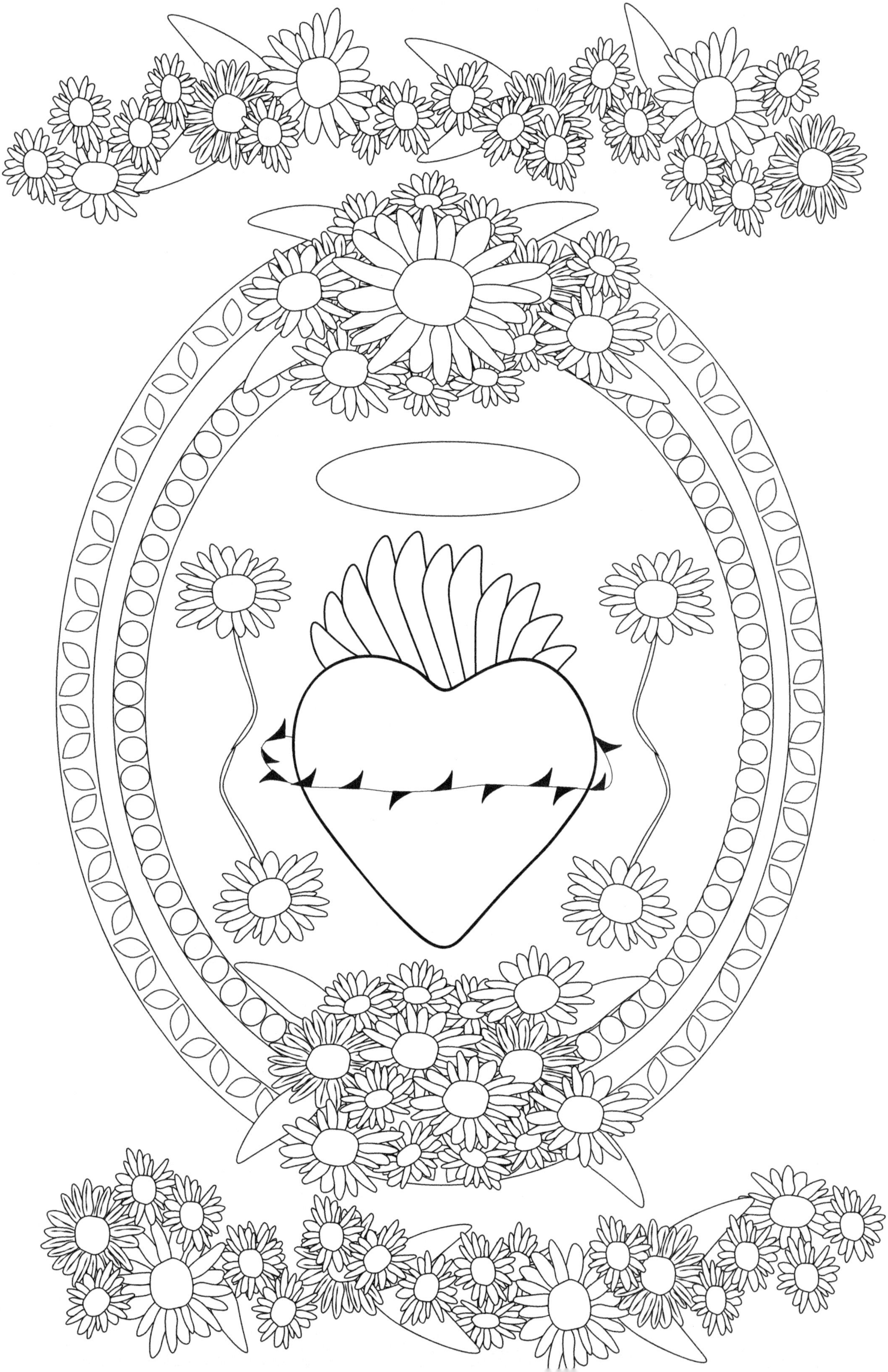

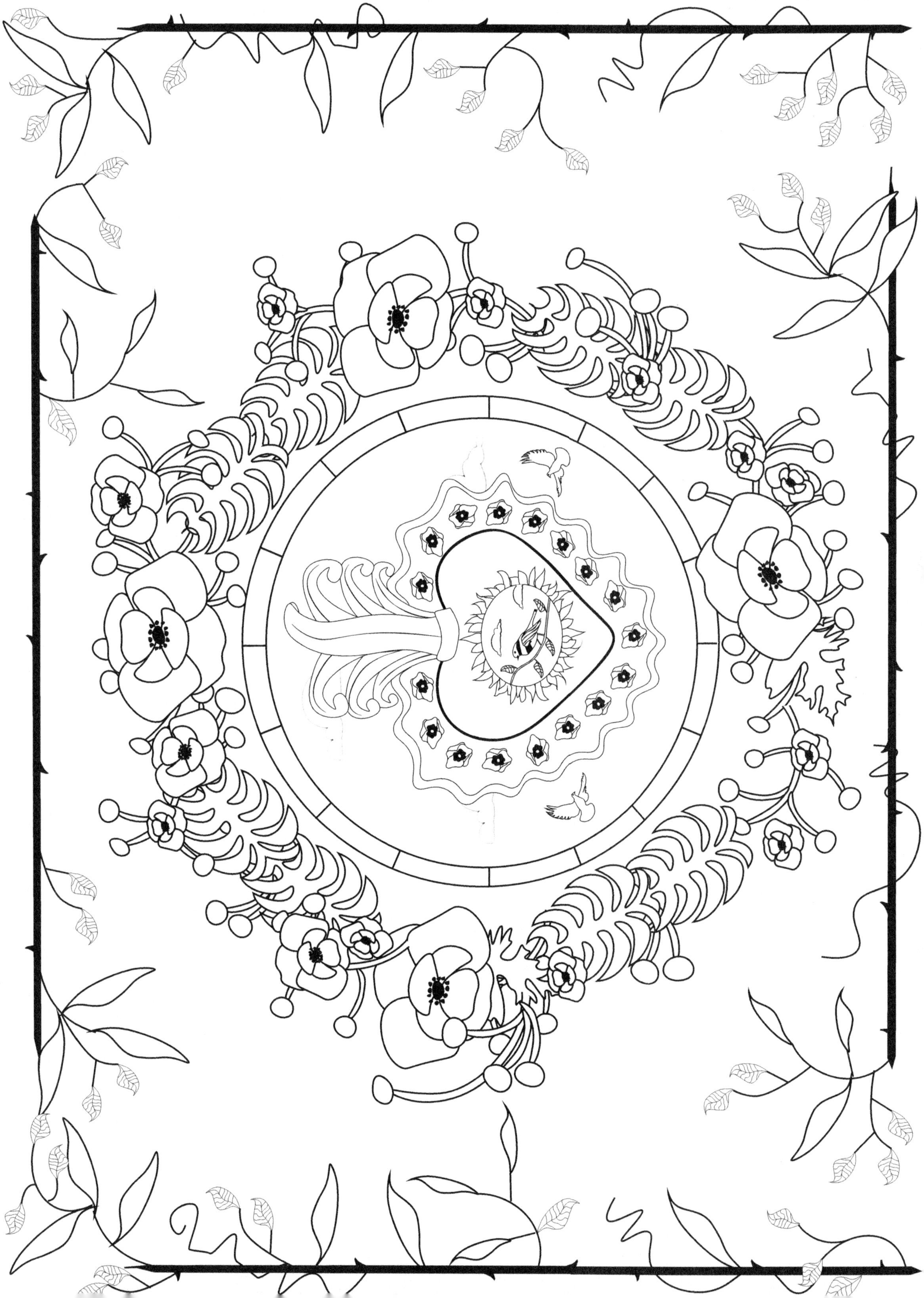

Printed in Great Britain
by Amazon